# The Smiling Photo

## Images of War

*It is my privilege to honor our Veterans for Peace with this gift*

## CAROLYN SNIVELY

*Carolyn Snively*

STONEYDALE PRESS PUBLISHING CO.

Stoneydale Press
523 Main Street
Stevensville, Montana 59870

*First Edition*

Library of Congress Control Number: 2012952695
Library of Congress Cataloging-in-Publication Data
Snively, Carolyn
The Smiling Photo, Images of War/Carolyn Snively
p. Cm.

Printed in the United States of America

ISBN 978-1-938707-01-8 (softcover)
ISBN 978-1-938707-02-5 (hardcover)

**Cover design and Illustrations by Timothy Botts**

To the women and men who dream of a world
where people honor each other
with love, justice and the olive branches of peace.

I wish to thank my friend Kimiko Connole, who encouraged my writing of Haiku, Lynda Smith and her valuable support, John Schlosser Jr., Linda Lussy and Margie Snively who read and offered excellent critiques and enthusiasm, my graphic photographer, Ron Williams, and my illustrator, Timothy Botts, whose beautiful background art complements the Haiku and speaks to the heart. My deepest thanks go to my husband John, for his constant support, love and patience.

Haiku is a form of Japanese poetry, dating from the 16th century; a three-lined seventeen-syllable poem, expressing a season, which may also refer to an age or an emotion. Classically, the first and third lines contain five syllables and the second has seven, but there are many acceptable exceptions to this rule. In THE SMILING PHOTO, the form of three lines has been altered to complement the artistic background by distinguishing the first word of each line with a capitalized letter.

In THE SMILING PHOTO, I have taken the liberty of using the Haiku form to depict the brutality that is visited upon soldiers and peoples in all wars.

War is a cruel and nasty business. The media chooses to portray the glory in victory or the valor in death, glossing over the victims of the war-torn country or the irreparable damage to the surviving military personnel. We do not see the family back home with the dead soldier's high school graduation or wedding picture smiling back at them. We do not see the broken soldier who returns with no quality of life left. We do not see the heartbreak of mothers who cannot feed their children. We do not see families who can never live in their land again. And we do not see the minds without conscience working to bring about devastation.

"A photograph is emblematic of
every story told about a fallen soldier."

Anonymous

"Poetry is to speak the unspeakable.
It's to say what's not to be said.
In that sense, it is sacred."

Sheryl Noethe, Montana's Poet Laureate

Wicked
thoughts
nurtured
In day time
become
night time
Birthing
grounds
for pain

One's
    integrity lies
In other minds;
    will justice
        Bloom or fade away

Cold eyes, hostile heart,
Silent voice; compromise has
Drifted
        beyond reach

A war's
ominous
Breath
blackens
the skies
with its
Putrid
stench
of death

Anguish
　　ripples from
One family
　　　to another
In waters
　　　of death

A man's head,
cradled
In rest;
eyes closed forever
While his buddy
screams

Unspoken fury
Tightens the throat;
seething spreads
From body to soul

Blinded anger plays
Music for
wanton dancing
Cheek to cheek
with death

Crosses litter paths
Of agony
where soldiers
Meet their
Golgotha

The lone note
      sustained
Burrows
      into the heart; door
            Of sorrow opens

Go away
    foul days;
Close the door
    to my
darkness;
    I wish only life

Homeless
hollow eyes
Stare at their
    sorry plight;
How could it
    get worse

Herded and
numbered,
Hearts hardened
like
shards
of ice;
Prisoners
of war

Empty stores
    of food
Cry like a
    mother's
dry breast;
    Bullets
    cannot feed

The smiling photo
Did not speak
of death to come;
Only life's summers

Fancies
of joy,
Muted
by reality,
Become
whispered
heartache

Wounded
    and wasted,
        The soldiers
    creep into their
            Winter
                of
                    despair

So much
anger in
Hearts that beat
above bellies
Longing
to be full

The mind
    must travel
Elsewhere
    when thoughts of the day
        Become too heavy

Honor
    Spring's body;
Memories
    from war
    hold thoughts
Of lost
    perfection

A shattered
building;
Dead
children;
young
soldiers
crying,
"God
what have
we done"

Angels' cries
fill the
Wailing wind;
only silent,
War-torn
bodies hear

Soldiers of sorrow
Dream of a nation's love;
An elusive myth

Behind closed eyes lives
A former life;
    now it lives
Only in daydreams

Sun's
streaking rays
Illuminate
another
cross;
Love lies
beneath

Can the
gentle winds
Of heaven
give lift
to hearts
So laden
with hate

Looking
    for goodness
In senseless evil,
  challenges
    The soul
      to forgive

Cries from the soul
Are answered in Heaven's echo;
"Time will gently heal"